# Vision in The Wilderness

## The Redemption

Carlton Bethley

# Acknowledgements …

I would like to acknowledge a few people who made the completion of this project a success for me… My wife who made herself available to listen to my rough drafts and hear out my concerns as I struggled with how to communicate them and always finding encouraging words that served as inspirational pushes for me…

Also My son who although is just 16 has been one of my biggest encouragers through his suggested time taker methods and his love for writing and reading with his eagerness to hear what has been written.. Thanks son for asking questions that most would consider beyond your years but had always been something that I considered to be apart of the brilliant mind and person that I know you to be.. Love You Beyond Comprehension – You are a World Changer a Difference Maker!!

Also thanks to Mark and Kayce Danos who have been the type of friends that very few are fortunate to have – I'm grateful for your friendship throughout the years and for how yall reached out to me during what would normally have been tough, and unbearable times to create avenues that coasted me to the other side.. An Irrefutable example that Character counts… The encouragement to be Optimistic and to finish Strong has proved to be fruitful in many ways… Your friendship is Priceless

Thanks to One Accord Ministry – Pastor Andy Pellarano has served as a True pastor and encourager- Has been the measuring Rod of Biblical Truth – A true example of the Passage "As iron sharpens Iron so does one man sharpens another: Proverbs 27:17 Your commitment to Outreach, helping others, and leadership has been an inspiration and push during some of the toughest and darkest moments of my Life- Thanks for being a Beacon of Light…

# Table of Contents

# THE ENCOUNTER

Captivated by the thought of being trapped in a Wilderness- My thoughts allow me to visualize the picture of a barren and lifeless place- one where the thirst would need quenched and hunger is a constant reality – How does one make it through such a period of time without dying of thirst or expiring due to hunger pains? Survival skills will fail us after so long – because the absence of life is just that The Absence of Life. I've learned that Divine Intervention and a super natural aide is the only thing that could get anyone through such a set of circumstances… Apparently God cared enough about us (the people of the World) to Pen a set of similar circumstances within the pages of the bible to give us an idea of how to get His attention through places that sometimes seem unbearable….There is a story in the bible that gives an example about a people who was called God's Chosen - immediately after their (Children of Israel) freedom from bondage – they were met with what seemed like an unbearable set of circumstances and it appeared impossible to get to the other side of it- but little did they know this would prove to be the beginning of the many lessons of Faith in the Wilderness that they would encounter…. Those who know the story know the story – those who don't – well I'll take a moment to explain a small version to give a general idea- The children of Israel were in captivity for over 400 years – for generation after generation all they knew was captivity and inhumane treatment after so long it became accepted as the norm… The majority of them had accepted their limited ability to be anything other than a slave- as a normal way of life… God divinely protected, developed, and raised up a man by the name of Moses- whom he would eventually speak to and through (Exodus 2-) in order to persuade Pharoah who at this time was The Leader of the Egyptians to free Israel after 400 years of enslavement… It eventually happened – he freed them after some supernatural arm twisting- but shortly after they were free they entered The Sinai Dessert to begin exploring their freedom – that did not come without the opposition of challenges. Pharoah shortly after changed his mind and decided to go after them … here's a Biblical passage that gives the full account of the story….

(Exodus Chapter 14 Moses and The COI Red Sea Encounter)

What happens next is Amazing because after Moses makes the decision to obey God against all odds IN THE WILDERNESS of Sinai something that had never happened took place- The Red Sea Opened up on both sides and allowed the Children of Israel to walk on dry land across to safety and as Pharoah's army attempted to follow them to attack – they were swallowed up and destroyed – not by the Children of Israel but by God – but only because they were obedient and trusted Him..

When I saw the Truth Revealed here- I was outdone of the treasure that was hid in this lesson – even though their way of life and culture had been stripped from them for 400 years – God sent an incredible message through that event- His message was plain and clear to me as I read the story. To me I saw God speaking to them- it was as if he was saying- I know you are in a place of unfamiliarity- but if you trust me the only one that can see what you can't see and can do what you can't do- I'll See You Through.

My very first time reading this story to the point of understanding was at the age of 18 while facing a life sentence in Prison. How I got to that point is a story within itself- I made some terrible decisions early in life that ultimately landed me there… However- while there I had a chance to ask myself some real questions. How did I get here? Understand me good- Not How did I get here- but HOW DID I GET HERE? As time went on that question was answered from a variety of angles. To make a long story short I will write about three different sets of wildernesses that I've had to encounter – it's my hope that simple basic truth will be painted picture clear and that the lesson that was displayed in the children of Israel very first obstacle in their Wilderness Journey would be magnified over and over again. The truth that is undoubtedly clear is that they were in an unfamiliar place- and were encountering unfamiliar circumstances yet them simply relying on God, learning how to hear His Voice, and knowing How to respond created an opportunity in order for them to arrive on the other side of what was about to be a complete disaster… How to avoid disaster within disaster is as simple as trusting God, hearing His voice and responding accordingly. There is no need to go into all the details but I will display some. The reason I was reading the story from a prison cell is because as a result of a prideful mindset I got into a fight with a guy that ended up terrible. The fight began over a position in a store line- something as simple as that. I can remember the guy cutting in front of me and the egotistical side of me rose up and said something to him about it- well he didn't like what was said and he said something back – and we got into an argument that led to the parking lot – we started fighting, he pulled a knife – not knowing that a pistol was in my possession. Yes I had a pistol- the environments (neighborhoods) that I was raised in and the people I was constantly surrounded by were of a toxic nature which means - I accumulated some very toxic habits and that one particularly landed me in prison facing a life sentence because when he came at me with the knife- I retrieved the pistol aimed and shot- The bullet unfortunately hit him in a vital spot that claimed his life later at the hospital. I was charged with Second degree murder. I was in the detective office talking with him while the guy was fighting for his life in the hospital and at this time my charge was attempted second degree murder but as we talked – someone came to the detectives office and beckoned for him to come out in the hall as if to share some information with him- which when he returned back in the office, I later found out that the information was that the guy had passed- which upgraded my charge from attempted to Second Degree Murder to Second Degree Murder. I remember for a second being in somewhat of a state of shock because that wasn't supposed to happen as I momentarily meditated on the reality of what happened- I came to the conclusion that my life had just been thrown away and kept saying to the detective as if in a trance my life is messed up, my life is messed up - and can remember him agreeing as he shook his head- Yep I must agree you've made a mess of things here…

Previous to the incident my work ethic from a very early age put me around some great people who grew to be like family to me… At the time of the incident I was employed as a Busboy at an Italian and Seafood restaurant in Monroe, la called The Chateau – had worked there from the age of 15 up until the incident at 18 and they absolutely Loved me as did I them. Mrs. Frankie Smith was head cook over there and when the incident happened

she called the jail and had them to give me a number to call her..
So I did and the conversation went as such-

Mrs. Frankie; how are you doing Carl? Are you ok? Do you need
anything? How are they treating you?

Me; I'm Ok- still processing everything

Mrs. Frankie: Carl – Do they have a church there?

Me: I hear they do

Mrs. Frankie: Give me your word – the next time they have it-
that you will go.. and if you need anything let us know

Me: Yes mam I will.. ( the only reason I went was because she
asked me to and I had given her my word- because to me I had
committed the unpardonable sin and felt God wouldn't want
anything to do with me)

I gave her my word that I would go and eventually went simply
because I gave her my word…

That was a conversation that I really needed to have – her voice,
the compassion and concern within it gave me the hope that people still cared about me even after what had happened. I knew I
wasn't a murderer but the fact of the matter that stood before me
was that someone lost their life at the hands of me – that would
be something I'm going to have to live with for the rest of my
life…

When Church call came

The guards came around and called for church – so I got up
and put on the jail issued cloths that was given me at the time
of booking and they led us to this place that was a room which

was used for multiple reasons… The perception of church to me at that time was this boring place where a preacher would come in and talk in an unexcited and boring tonic way that's all it was – there was no real relevance or significance -after all I was only there because I gave Mrs. Frankie my word that I would go… However the tables turned when this preacher started speaking – he started off a little slow at first but then he captivated me with the stories he began to share and he talked about things that pertained to my life from when I was knee high clean on up to that particular point – I was out done- He gave an altar call but I didn't go. Once the service was over- I laid on my bunk and thought about everything that was said and immediately it was like I had an epiphany – God was speaking through the preacher letting me know that I had not committed the unpardonable sin and that a second chance was available for me… I got out of my bunk and kneeled on my knees and asked God if I could have a second shot at life and living. I told him if Jesus died for me to create away for me to have a relationship with you – I want it and need it- I asked Him to Help me- Help me with this situation and Help me be a better person Lord.. Shortly after that prayer I began to hunger for the knowledge of Who I was as person and why was I here on earth- The topic of Life and Death took on a whole new meaning to me- I need-ed to know my life beyond this point could be purposeful….. I was told that the bible contained information that could help me discover Who I was in God's sight- that if I read, studied, and applied it to my life- The Creator's Purpose would be unfolded to me and that I could live life beyond this point as God's son and He as My Father… When hearing He designed a purpose for my life that no one else on earth could fulfill but me - hearing information like that made me want to know more about it so

I started reading the bible every day… One of the most mind boggling, yet inspiring things I learned was that as big as God is and as Awesome as He is He created a specific identity designed solely for me..

Shortly after this something happened in The Wilderness of Prison that I didn't expect- the detective who was over the case created something I was never supposed to get and that was a preliminary hearing… At this hearing he would get on the stand and testify on my behalf- I could remember his testimony as if it was yesterday he said "The victim at one point in the incident was the aggressor towards Carlton with a dangerous weapon and Carlton responded in the manner that he did because he felt his life was in danger… As a result of his testimony they dropped the charge from Second degree Murder to manslaughter and the bond went from 200,000 to 50,000 this was a big break for me because what it said to me was – one day I'll be free again.. Ultimately I ended up getting a 21 year sentence where I served 10 years 3 months 7 days and 8 hours .. As I look back on God touching the heart of the detective was a Spiritual Red Sea for me because through the detectives testimony it gave me an out date something to look forward to.. The task I had now was I just had to rely on God to develop me during my stay there to be the best version of who He created me to be as the time drew near and that would prove to be a task within itself – because there were episode after episode that proved to be growing pains …

# THE WILDERNESS

Doing time in prison was a task within itself – because although I had given and committed my life to God to follow the ways and teachings of Jesus – the fact of the matter is – I was still in prison- a place where people thrived on survival.. Many of the guys there with me had burned several bridges with their families and friends- so all they had in life was the circumstances of the environment and in their mind it was necessary that they used the circumstances to survive the best way they could and that could mean anything.. So although my heart and my spirit had been redeemed by the blood of the lamb – it was vital that I use my mind while it was consistently being renewed, refreshed, and revised to navigate through this very dangerous environment.. Respect and Disrespect were very big in the element of prison and you always had someone who would test what they could get away with and what they couldn't- What you allowed- you allowed, and what you didn't – you didn't- simple as that- and Not allowing something could mean taking the ultimate stand.. Nevertheless even with all of this being true- I was determined to draw my lines of what I deemed Respect and disrespect and grow in Christ within those boundaries and Trust God that no one crossed them… In 10 years some of those lines were slightly crossed and some even edged a little and there were stands that had to be taken – none of them got too far out of hand Thank God- but there were some that became shockers to the scenario in the present moment.. Ill share them later in the book…

One of the things that I found to be true once I got to prison was that there were many people from different areas of the state that had made the same commitment to God and had a similar analytical strategy that I had committed to in order to grow as a person in a very dangerous environment.. When these guys became obviously recognizable – there were brotherhood bonds that were formed and still exist even til this day… There were people such as Speedy, O.G. Bobby Sneed, Shaveen Hill, Fabian Logwood- who had made a Pitt-bull grip commitment to change for betterment of themselves through Biblical principles… We would have bible studies together and one of the things that I believe helped us grow tremendously in an environment such as that was the fact that we recognized each others different views of the same truth.. It didn't change the truth – we were just in a position to learn that there are many ways to look at the same Truth and none of it changes the fact that The Truth is The Truth… These were people who had been deemed dangerous by society and a threat to the community – but we chose to believe something different about ourselves and the mirror that we looked in everyday to remind us of how we're viewed by God was the bible.. We didn't use cliché quotes- we sought out hidden truths in the bible and shared them with excitement with each other….Information that showed us why we could be forgiven, why we had second chances to be Blessed in and out of where we were - but not just that- we learned information that would place us on a path to destiny, a path of purpose and aim.. We challenged and sharpened each other towards the attainment of those tools and equipment… Godly wisdom and knowledge became to us as protective equipment is to the Fireman, Marine-men, or Policeman.. It became like a shield for our mind, soul, and spirit to help us maneuver through the dangers of the environment…

I can remember one day while in the Leather Hobby shop – Speedy (whose real name is Oliver Miles) and I were in there along with many others that were there- we were both working on separate projects. Speedy was very talented from a musical standpoint and all of a sudden he started singing this song that came to him and I can remember it just like it was yesterday "Bought it Bought it For The Lord- I won't turn back because I'm bought it bought it for the Lord" He like got into a lil zone and started singing it with the peppiest hip hop beat- and the spirit of that song transcended that day – because it became a part of my view… I had the thought- If I was Bought it Bought it in the streets for all the wrong reasons- how much more could I be Bought it Bought it for God and every reason that's good… Bought it Bought it was a term or phrase that's used in the hood from a negative standpoint to depict that whatever is about to happen in this present moment I'm ready to meet it with what-ever force is necessary.. I saw how that could be used with my desire to please God and carryout a purpose that honors the im-age of Who God is…

O.G. Bobby Sneed – Well we didn't really call him O.G. which in Street terms means Original Gangster … Its just that Bob-by reminds me of a character that played in the Movie called "South Central" O.G. Bobby Johnson was the movie characters name… and their stories are quite similar… Fortunately in the real life version of Sneed's- others and myself get the opportuni-ty to see the extended version, which came with Bobby getting out of prison and becoming active in his son's ( L' Jarius Sneed) life watching and being instrumental in many ways him become a phenomenal athlete through college and ultimately getting that one shot that many great athletes dream of but very seldom get the opportunity to experience… L' Jarius was drafted in 2020 by the Kansas City Chiefs to the National Football League and for the last couple years through his hard work and dedication has shown and proven that he deserve to be there by earning many accolades, one that created a dispute that he arguably deserved the "Mack Hill Rookie of The Year " award.. I can remember while on the inside of prison Bobby came up with a song that was literally scripture – I mean scripture scripture – I will never look at Psalm 64 the same again after I heard Bobby sing the song the way he did… He sung Psalm 64 which says "Hear My Voice O God of my prayer, preserve my life from fear of the enemy- hide me from the secret counsel of the wicked, from the insurrection of the workers of iniquity- who wet their tongue like a sword and like a bended arrow" The song was actually a prayer and the content within that prayer was explosive to me because it was the prayer of David – who literally was protected by God from all that he mentioned within the prayer… Although Bobby introduced me to the prayer in that way- it became my prayer and my thoughts every time I encounter opposition that has no real reason the only reason it forms is to hinder progress… As for Bobby- I guess the term O.G. took on another meaning from his perspective – he changed the Game of his life, made some adjustments that impacted his son as well in a positive way- if you ask me and no one is but id say Bobby is an Original Game Changer ….

Then you had Shaven Hill.. When Hill committed His life to God… he had this unashamed zeal about himself that just wanted everyone to know The God that changed his life and there was an evangelistic spirit about him that led him into the yards of the facilities just talking and sharing his faith about Who God was to him and why he thought everyone should know Jesus… As the inmate Pastor of the facility The Lord led me to give him an opportunity to share a message – because he had proven himself to be a man of faith with compassion for others.. I remember the message like it was yesterday – the title of it was "I Go A Fishing" To this day it remains one of the most inspiring messages I have ever heard among the brinks of evangelism.. He was from South Louisiana in an area that has some of the greatest fishing arenas- he used his upbringing around fishing to expound in a detailed manner from a biblical standpoint and phrase of Jesus 'I will make you fishers of men" .. His passion and fire around this topic was reigniting of mine and even today I'm always reverting back to that message when I ask myself Why should we be fishers of Men? Why should we care about people in a way that causes us to Reach Out?

F.L. if I could write a book about this guy I would.. He's from my home town and arguably was the most or one of the most respected guys on the streets in the city of Monroe during that time.. I had heard stories about him for a long time from relatives, and just the streets in general- but I had never actually physically saw him in person… So when he came to the facility – everyone put out the word to the people that were from our area that he had made it… When he came into the setting where I was at- I'm looking for this Big Suge Knight looking fellow but that wasn't the case.. he walked up to me and shook my hand- and to my surprise his hands were smooth as if he had never really worked a day in his life… he was an interesting fellow.. I thought man I'd like to get to know this guy but of course I'm not going to run up behind him like a pawn- although there were many that did.. My thought frame was - he put on his pants the same way I put on mine- he do his time – I do mine…. At one point we ended up in the same dorm together and every night at the end of the night – we (a group of men in the same dorm) had formed a prayer meeting every night where we would gather for a group prayer before we went to sleep and he would always come- share his prayer request and we'd pray.. I gradually got to know him through making small talk – we were from the same area- he went to school and played football with my oldest cousin Charles Mcfarland - so that gave us conversation grounds… One of the things that I learned about him was- he had a lot of college education- very very intelligent guy… At some point we actually became friends- some of the same people within the facility that I had gravitated towards he gravitated towards also so many of our friends were mutual – maybe that had something to do with it.. There were times I would look over by his bunk and he'd be on his knees praying and it was a testament to me because I was aware of the power he possessed on the street.. Then it dawned on me- he didn't possess that power and influential pull because of his ability to over power people physically.. He was a thinker and could out think the best – I liked being around people who were great thinkers because you can always learn something from them.. One of the things I've learned about Great Thinkers- if they allow you within their circle – most of them don't mind sharing their thoughts or how their thoughts came to be… To make a long story short F.L. allowed me to pick his brain a lot and there were times of course he laughed at me while I did it because I could ask some of the craziest questions- nevertheless he became a brother and a friend…

# THE FRUIT

I mentioned earlier how Great thinkers in many cases are eager
to share their information with people who they believe would
use it and benefit from… I began working for an Offshore company about 3 ½ years after I came home  Working for an oil-
field/offshore company was something I always wanted to do
because before my Culinary Arts course was completed – the
school put on what we called a Job Fair –a lot of emphasis at the
fair was placed on how culinary skills are valued in the Offshore
arena.. So upon the conception of that idea – it had always been
a thought and desire in which id ponder from time to time …
Finally I got a break- a guy by the name of G-Hop (Gary Hop-
kins ) – one that I had been incarcerated with shortly before I
came home.. During our incarceration Gary and I became good
friends and I mentioned to him about my desire to work in the
offshore arena- in which it was a desire of his as well.. Gary and
I kept in contact with each other upon our release and he ended
up in the Offshore arena working for a great company and while
there he remembered the conversation we had and called me
and told me the company was a good one and thought id fit well
there… He provided the information that I needed and not long
after following through on it a call came through… The guy on
the other end name was Paul Robichaux- I remember the conversation like yesterday.. He asked me if I could be in the Larose
area tomorrow by 10:00 the next morning.. Larose is deep south

from where I resided- actually 5 hours south of Monroe… At this time I was driving tow trucks in the West Monroe area and was doing pretty well but in my mind working for an Offshore company displaying my culinary skills is where I always wanted to be… therefore I explained to Mr. Paul that I'm with this company and I'd like to at least give them a week notice before up and dragging out on them… Paul was very honest with me and said- Carlton that is very commendable, in fact – you're just the type of person we'd love to have on board because of your consideration in that manner. However, I have to be honest with you- I can't promise you that the position would be still open at that time- but it is Now. I gave it some thought understanding that this opportunity may not be available for long- being at sort of a cross road- I had to make the decision that was best for me and my family- and for many reasons this New Opportunity is what I believed was best for me and mine… I told Paul – see you tomorrow at 10 and we gracefully hung up.. I immediately called the owner of the tow truck company and explained to him about the conversation I just had and what I was considering… He told me he'd be right over- and that he did- his first question was- What would I have to do to keep you… I had heard of other people being at this point where they could name their price- it dawned on me that my skill had placed me in a position of demand- I was valued and Mr. Ricky was willing to play tug-a-war but Danos pull on me was just a little more stronger and stern- as they were offering 1000.00 a week plus benefits and when I told Mr. Ricky that- his response was "WELLL- If I had that opportunity – id probably take it to".. They wished me well Long story short – I ended up in Larose that next morning to began my journey with the best company I have had the privilege of working with ever… Once I got the shot and the opportunity – it was up to me to assure them they made the right decision and their forefront worker at the reception desk when I came in was name Mrs. Sarah.. She saw how excited I was to get the opportunity and dropped a nugget of advice in my bucket to carry with me… Mrs. Sarah said – remember these two words and you'll be ok "PLAY BALL" … So I asked her what did that mean and she explained the company prided itself on being a Team- which meant that if asked to do something that may not be a direct job description duty but necessary at the time – get it done for the benefit of the team.. I Liked the idea of the theme and pondered it in my mind… I was there to actually be a rigger (entrance level) and was planning on working my way up towards the kitchen but something incredible happen.. I had brought all of my certifications the ones from prison and everything- and the Culinary Arts Diploma had "Winn Correctional Center" on it as big as day.. yet when Paul saw it- all he saw was the grades, the skill, and the need they had at the present moment… he came back in the room where I was with a high level of excitement and told me he had a spot for me that pays more then the original and had some leverages and if I wanted the position – it was mine and I can start immediately.. Of course without question- I accepted the position as Cook/ Bunkhouse manager and served them for 13 years… I did not hesitate to put Sarah's Play Ball theme to work once I got settled and figured out how things operated.. When I would learn that a helper was needed at the Fabrication shop on my shift off- I would recommend myself- it was extra money and I was around people and places I could learn from… Other company personel got word that the cook was willing on his time off to fill in the gap where needed- this helped them and this helped me… They would send me to get all kind of certifications Fork lift certifications- when they needed extra transportation help- they would send me to Defensive driving courses so that I could have every certification needed.. At one point Mr. Hank asked how I felt about sharing my testimony with staff- of course I'm always amped to share my testimony – I'm one of those people that believe that we are overcomers by the blood and the Word of our Testimony as the scripture says (Revelation 12:11)- so without question I did it. At one point I was a little leery before sharing but God gave me self-control and I was able to speak with confidence and a good demeanor which made for an excellent delivery and a great reception… One of my fill in the gap moments was I had to take/transport Mr. Hank- owner of the company from Larose to Baton Rouge… I remember thinking to myself-all this wisdom, success, and experience in here with me and there's an opportunity to ask key questions- its my fault if I let it pass by.. I also remember thinking – he may think I'm completely crazy and fire me on the spot… However, if that happened- I still have God and that is enough.. So I went in- Mr. Hank- can I ask you a question? He was like sure what's the question.. I said- if you had to say- What would say would be the Key to your success? He looked at me and said Carlton you know more people should ask questions like that and he gave me an honest solid answer… He said I can't say that its one particular key- it's a series of many keys- my first contribution I would say started when I gave my life to God as a senior in High School and then from that discipline was a very high factor- because I had friends that were doing things that I wanted to do and going places that I wanted to go but because I disciplined myself and chose not to- it had a higher reward down the pipe…. Those Words stuck with me down the pipe and since my conversation that day and many other days I've seen the fruit from it in so many areas- plus I got to keep my job and earned his respect in a way that was never even sought… To Add wood to the fire of my previous thought that Great Thinkers look for opportunity to share their thoughts with people whom they feel will use them and benefit from it…

Landing the job with Danos helped me to build many job related relationships with the different people I interacted with. I was blessed to come in contact with some brilliant people – just to name some people such as David Poe , Jose, and Elvira… David Poe was just brilliant and was a wealth of knowledge just walking.. There were times I would have to pick David up from the airport – he was heading up a program in Africa which is a place I'd love to go and really thought that the opportunity would present itself for me to go through the company- but that time with the company never came.. However my hopes of going to Africa still is very much alive… when I would pick David up from the Airport which was near an hour drive away- once in the car he would talk non-stop from the airport until we arrived at the office… here's the kicker (or excellency of it all) even though he talked non-stop until we got to the office there was never a boring conversation… he was always thinking- We'd pass by a house with a certain type of roof on it and he would explain what type of roof it was- how good the quality of it was or was not… Anytime I knew that David needed to be picked up – id be eager to pick him up because I knew he would talk about things that I could learn from… The other two that I'd love to pick up was Elvira and Jose - I looked for the opportunity to pick them up because they were actually from Africa – a place of my ancestors origin and to be in the car with them with opportunity to ask questions was special.. Elvira was very talkative about her upbringing and the role she played with her other siblings- for she was the oldest – and had to make sacrifices that would be considered abnormal to the average American.. Those sacrifices placed her in a position to become a key factor for her family and created an avenue for her siblings and future generations to walk through.. she has a very impressive story… Jose he was a lil more reluctant – yet inquisitive but very attentive in our conversation.. It took a minute for him to become comfortable with who I was as a person and black man but the ice did break… I remember picking him up during a time where a lot was going on over here in the states from a racially pressured stand point… We engaged in a conversation on the topic and sometimes you have to be careful when talking about such topics especially with office personnel- however I felt comfortable enough to talk with Jose about it and it turned out well… Our most evoking conversation was when we discussed the difference and importance of being culturally aware and properly informed and culturally dead or ignorant… Very fruitful conversation -he was a stern guy and very family oriented and believed in cultivating culture- It was a delight to meet such incredible people along my journey. I've just listed a few there are so many more stories of so many others I could share story after story..

Once I realized that Danos would be a place id be for a significant amount of time. I started looking for places to stay/ Rent to reside I wanted to live here – I was comfortable with my environment and was around a completely different type of culture- It was progressive, it was Functional, and it encouraged Growth and structure… I eventually moved to the New Orleans area which was about 45 minutes from the work site- definitely was a shorter ride then 5 hours… I was careful in making the decision because New Orleans had its own reputation. However- through work I got a chance to mingle with some people while filling in the gap as a Fork Lift operator on the Westbank in Harvey- enough to discover that The City of New Orleans is a very beautiful place…. As a runner I saw that an upcoming 10k event would be happening in the city- The event was titled The Crescent City Classic.. It's a 6.2 mile run/jog through a beautiful and scenic area of the City.. Once I did that run and visited the different parks, aquariums, restaurants- I was sold on the city.. The Culture of the City for me out weighed the dangers that without doubt existed as well.. However, My mind set was if you're going to live life and enjoy it- you can't be scared to take risk- you can't live in fear… ( for God has not given us the Spirit of Fear but of Power, Love, and a Sound Mind)- So I moved to New Orleans and it was one of the better decisions I've made… I've met incredible people from all walks of life – and the opportunity opened up for me to do mission trips to Guatemala through 1st Baptist Church of Avondale – Great Church and Great people - they would pay for my flight round trip- I never in my wildest imagination saw this happening but it did and all I could say was God I See You- so I embraced the opportunity and had a phenomenal time and made some monumental memories as the pictures below would show…

Pastor Mark Daniels is a very wise, intelligent and great teacher and believed in following the Lead of God's Spirit many times against his better judgment because he knew enough to know that God knows best. He would engage in conversation with me and as it would have it he discovered my love for outreach in various of areas such as prison ministry. I had expressed to him my involvement within it before moving to New Orleans with David Oatis of Lifeline Prison and Outreach Ministry, and Pastor Don Banks of Greater Realness Outreach in Monroe, La- and my desire to do it here in New Orleans. Needless to say he never forgot that conversation- and when something came across his desk about a Big Prison Ministry team coming to New Orleans looking for people to help and assist... He asked me to come to his office he wanted to talk to me... Once in his office he showed me the flyer about the prison ministry and said to me – to be honest I'm not into prison ministry but I know you are and thought that this would be something you'd be interested in as he handed me the flyer. I was appalled at his honesty – a little curious as to why he wouldn't be interested in prison ministry- but overwhelmed that he thought enough about it to consider me. I reckoned he had his hand in so much in a variety of areas that another ministry could become burdensome- but he handed the ball off to me- and boy did I score with this one. I called the number and they gave me the location of the next meeting and when I showed up- of course there was a moment where everyone had to introduce themselves and explain why they are interested in going into the prison. After the committee of the Bill Glass Prison and Outreach Ministry heard my testimony and learned who I was – it seemed overnight I became like this poster child for this event in this area… After that meeting every meeting Going forward for that event – would not start unless I gave a 5 min. word of exhortation Mr. Rick Blair who was the facilitator was very adamant about that… and there were times when I would come in a little late and the meeting would stop and would not proceed because they were anxious to hear the 5 min. exhortation… I was full of what's called popcorn exhortations and always found a way to bring the relevancy back to the moment… The event was Phenomenal and all of the episodes leading up to it. We had a banquet not long before the event was to happen and I met one of the chaplains from the areas who approached me after I shared a brief reason for why I was there and what it meant to me. Chaplain Kathy Radke Roberts who was the Chaplain for the Jefferson Parish area-if you know anything about Jefferson Parish then you know it makes a circle around the Orleans Parish and is considered a very dangerous area. She told me about her prison/jail facilities and asked if I would be interested in coming and speaking to her Youth at the Detention

Center- Of course I said yes because of the level of passion that I possessed towards sounding the horn for our Youth as an effort to prevent them from going further down the road. That was the Birth of a really good friendship/relationship with Chaplain Kathy and her husband Robert- and open the door for me to serve there throughout the years- Covid put a strain on things but I'm still waiting to get back in there- such a rewarding area of service.

Reverting back to the Bill Glass Prison Ministry- once we did New Orleans – I was asked to do another one in Shreveport with them and one of my Greatest ventures with them was the one in Kansas. They flew me out to Wichita, Kansas for a Banquet there and we had a Phenomenal time met some incredible people – got a chance to sit and hang out with Tully Blanchard one of the four horsemen back when wrestling was very entertaining. Tully was a guy whose heart was just as big as he was and he loved Jesus and it showed in his commitment to see the events through… The name of the Events that we were doing was called Weekend for Champions and I was surrounded by literally retired Champions and some not retired – they teamed us up in teams of two and I was teamed up with a man who was in the genius world book of records his name was Big James Henderson they called him Hollywood, he had done movies with the likes of Chuck Norris, and he was also the first man to bench Press over 700lbs raw without any substance assistance… Big James was a giant of a man with a heart as enormous as he was- and to top it off- his skill for speaking was beyond unique and powerful- his ability to communicate with his strength and his voice was amazing to me and because I was teamed up with him for the whole weekend- I was able to pull and learn from him… He was a natural mentor- as we would eat lunch – he would allow me to ask questions- and he would give pointers that proved to be effective there but more so throughout the years afterwards.

These were just some of the experiences that became unforgettable because of the type of environment- I was allowed in- and as I think about it even today- I was amongst so many champions, Bench Press Champions, World Renown Ventriloquist, Football Champions- all of these champions that loved Jesus- and the more I thought about it led me to ask a real question to myself. How did I get chosen to be around so many champions that Love Jesus- What made me significantly standout to be amongst so many great people- and it dawned on me as a former inmate who dealt with against the odd circumstances- because I chose to trust Jesus through the Wilderness of Prison process – I became a Champion over my circumstances….,.. Glory To God!!! We Are really True Champions when we trust The Greatest Champion of All Time Jesus Christ…..

I'd Like to end this book with a prayer in hopes that my readers understand the importance, and the value of life, that they may know- one decision can change your life for the betterment and can put you in a position where you can grow by leaps and bounds- however one bad decision can cause you to lose everything within the snap of a finger.. The difference is measuring how to make good decisions and how to make bad decisions. I can only tell and share what happened for me – and what happened for me was that I made a decision to trust God through Jesus the Christ and from there – I began to grow from within- learning the nature of who I was and am as a man and exploring and experiencing communication with God….

My Prayer For You

God May Everyone that reads this book- find a Peace that can only come from You. I Trust you to Speak to their hearts and Increase their desire to learn of You and that you would Inspire them to measure Who they are through the revelation of your Word… Equip them with the tools to develop, sharpen and release the many gifts and talents that most times are hidden until you shine Your light on them..

In the name of Jesus The Christ Amen

www.ingramcontent.com/pod-product-compliance
Lightning Source LLC
Chambersburg PA
CBHW051408150726
48000CB00003B/1378